The Great Songs Of
The Kinks

Published by
Hal Leonard

Exclusive distributors:

Hal Leonard
7777 West Bluemound Road
Milwaukee, WI 53213
Email: info@halleonard.com

Hal Leonard Europe Limited
42 Wigmore Street
Marylebone, London, W1U 2RN
Email: info@halleonardeurope.com

Hal Leonard Australia Pty. Ltd.
4 Lentara Court
Cheltenham, Victoria, 3192 Australia
Email: info@halleonard.com.au

Order No.AM964051
ISBN 978-0-7119-8175-6
This book © Copyright 2000 by Hal Leonard

Book design by Phil Levene

Cover photograph courtesy of Rex Features
Compiled by Peter Evans

www.halleonard.com

All Day And All Of The Night

Words & Music by Ray Davies

B♭ G F G F B♭ G F
be with you all of the time. The
B♭ F A G
on - ly time I feel al - right is by your side.
C A D C F D C
Girl I want to be with you all of the
D C F D C D C
time, all day and all of the night. All day and

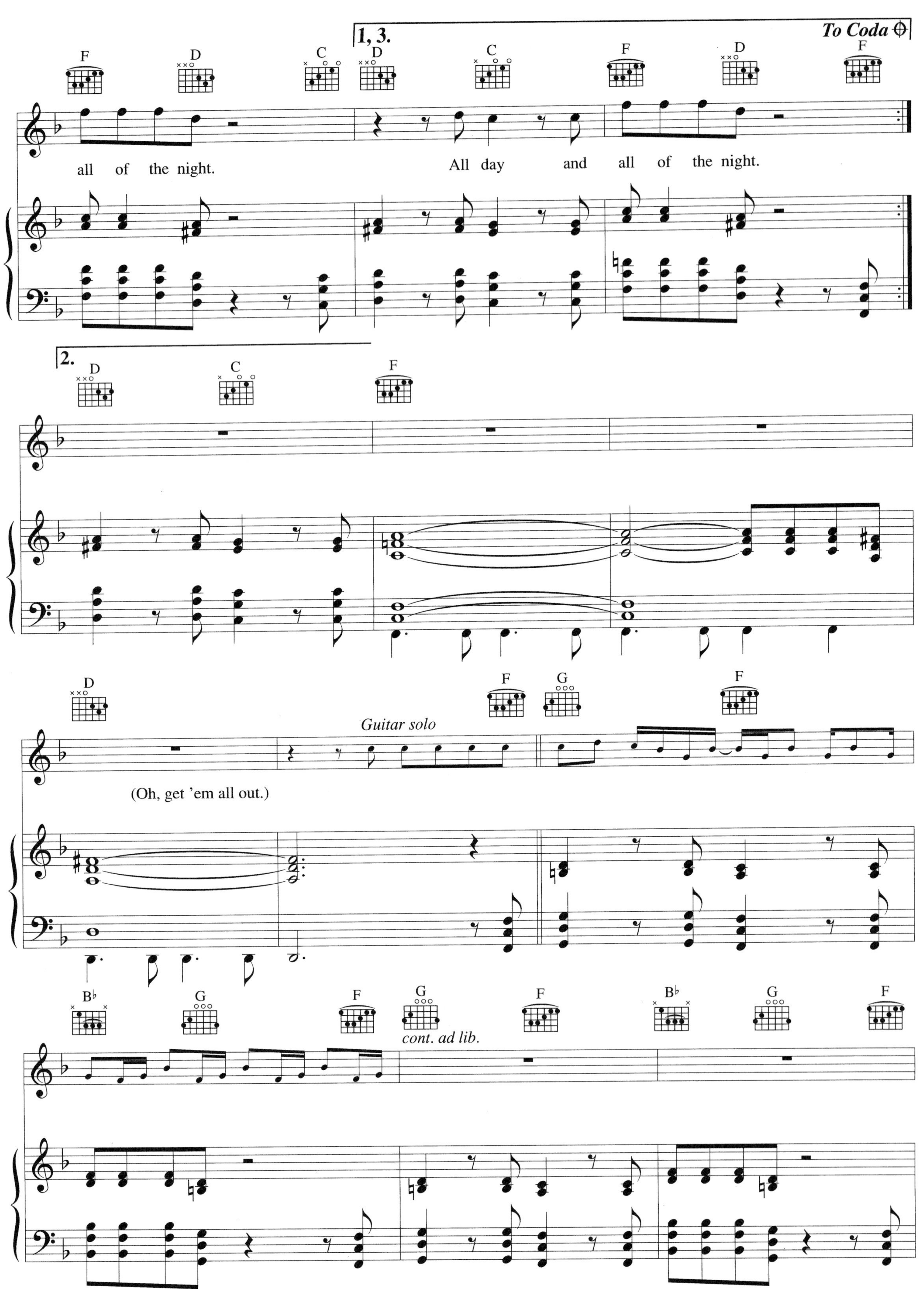

1, 3.
To Coda
F   D   C   D   C   F   D   F
all of the night.
All day   and   all of the night.
2.
D   C   F
D
Guitar solo
(Oh, get 'em all out.)
B♭   G   F   G   F   B♭   G   F
cont. ad lib.

D.%. al Coda

Coda

Verses 2 & 3:
I believe that you and me'll last forever
Oh yeah, all day and night I'm yours, leave me never.

The only time I feel alright *etc*.

Apeman

Words & Music by Ray Davies

E7
D
walk-ing round like flies man; So Im no bet-ter than the an-i-mals sit-ting in their
A
ca-ges in the zoo man 'Cos com-pared to the flow-ers and the birds and the trees
E7
A
A
I am an ape-man I think Im so ed-u-ca-ted and Im so civ-il-ised, 'cos Im a
(Spoken) In man's evolution he has created
A

E7
A
strict veg-e-tar-i-an   And with the
the cities and the motor traffic rumble,
ov-er pop-u-la-tion and in-fla-tion and star-va-tion,and the
but give me half a chance and I'd be taking off my

E7
D
cra-zy pol-i-tic-i-ans___
clothes and living in the jungle (Sung) But the
I don't feel safe in this world no more___ I
on-ly time   that I   feel at ease___ is

A
don't want to die in a nuc-le-ar war
swing-ing up and down in a co-co-nut tree
I want to sail a-way to a dis-tant shore and
Oh what a life of lux-u-ry to

E7
A
CHORUS
make like an ape man.
be like an ape man.
I'm an ape man, I'm an ape, ape man oh I'm an

E7
A
ape man.
I'm a king-kong man, I'm a voo-doo man oh I'm a
E7
D
ape-man.
'Cos com-pared to the sun that sits in the sky, com-
I look out the win-dow, but I can't see the sky, 'cos
A
- pared to the clouds as they roll by, com-pared to the bugs and the spi-ders and flies
air po-lu-tion is a fogging up my eyes, I want to get out of this ci-ty a-live and
E7
A
D
Amaj7
I am an ape man.
La la la__ la la__ la la__
make like an ape man.

E7
A
E7
A
E7
A
E7
A
A
E7
la la la la
la la la la Come on and love
me, be my ape man girl and we'll be so
hap-py in my ape man world.
I'm an ape man, I'm an ape, ape man oh I'm an ape man
I'm a

A
E7
king kong man, I'm a voo doo man oh I'm an ape man.
I
A
I'll be your Tar - zan you'll be my Jane   I'll keep you warm and you'll keep me sane, We'll
don't feel safe in this world no more,   I don't want to die in a nuc-le-ar war___ I
D
1 E7   A
sit   in the trees and eat ba-na-nas all day   just like an ape man.
want to sail a-way   to a dif-frent shore, and
2 E7   A   D   Amaj7   E7   A
make like an ape man.   La la la__ la la la la__   la la__ la la__

Arthur

Words & Music by Ray Davies

© Copyright 1969 Davray Music Limited.
Carlin Music Corporation, Iron Bridge House, 3 Bridge Approach, London NW1.
All Rights Reserved. International Copyright Secured.

14

G   D7
All the way he was o-ver-tak-en by peo-ple who make the big de-
How's your life and your Shan-gri-La and your long lost land of Hal-le-

G
ci-sions; But he tried and he tried for a bet-ter life And a
lu-jah; And your hope and glo-ry has passed you by, Can't you

D7   G
way to im-prove his own con-di-tion. If
see what the world is do-in' to ya. And

C   G   F
on-ly life were eas-y, it would be such fun;
now we see your chil-dren sail-in' off in the set-ting sun;

Things would be more e - qual and be
To a new ho - ri - zon where there's
plen - ty for ev - 'ry - one.
plen - ty for ev - 'ry - one.
Ar -thur, the world's gone and passed you by, Don't you know it? Don't you
Ar -thur, could be that the world was wrong, Don't you know it? Don't you
Ar -thur, the world's gone and passed you by, Don't you know it? Don't you
know it? You can cry, cry all night, but it won't make it right, Don't you
know it? Ar -thur, could be you were right all a -long, Don't you
know it? You can cry, cry all night, but it won't make it right, Don't you

G7
C
know it?______ Don't you know it?______ Ar-thur, we know and we
know it?______ Don't you know it?______ Now____ we know and we
know it?______ Don't you know it?______ Ar-thur, we read you and

G7
C
sym - pa - thize, Don't you know it?______ Don't you know it?______
sym - pa - thize, (Tacet)________________________________
un - der - stand you, (Tacet)________________________________

Ar - thur, we like you and want to help you,
We'd like to help you and un - der - stand you,
Ar - thur, we read you and un - der - stand you,

G7
1 C
Some - bod - y loves you, don't you know it?
(Tacet)______________________________
(Tacet)______________________________

2
C
G7
Don't you know it? Don't you
C
G7
know it? Some - bod - y loves you, don't you
C
G7
know it? Don't you know it? Don't you
C
G7
C
know it?
D. S. al Coda

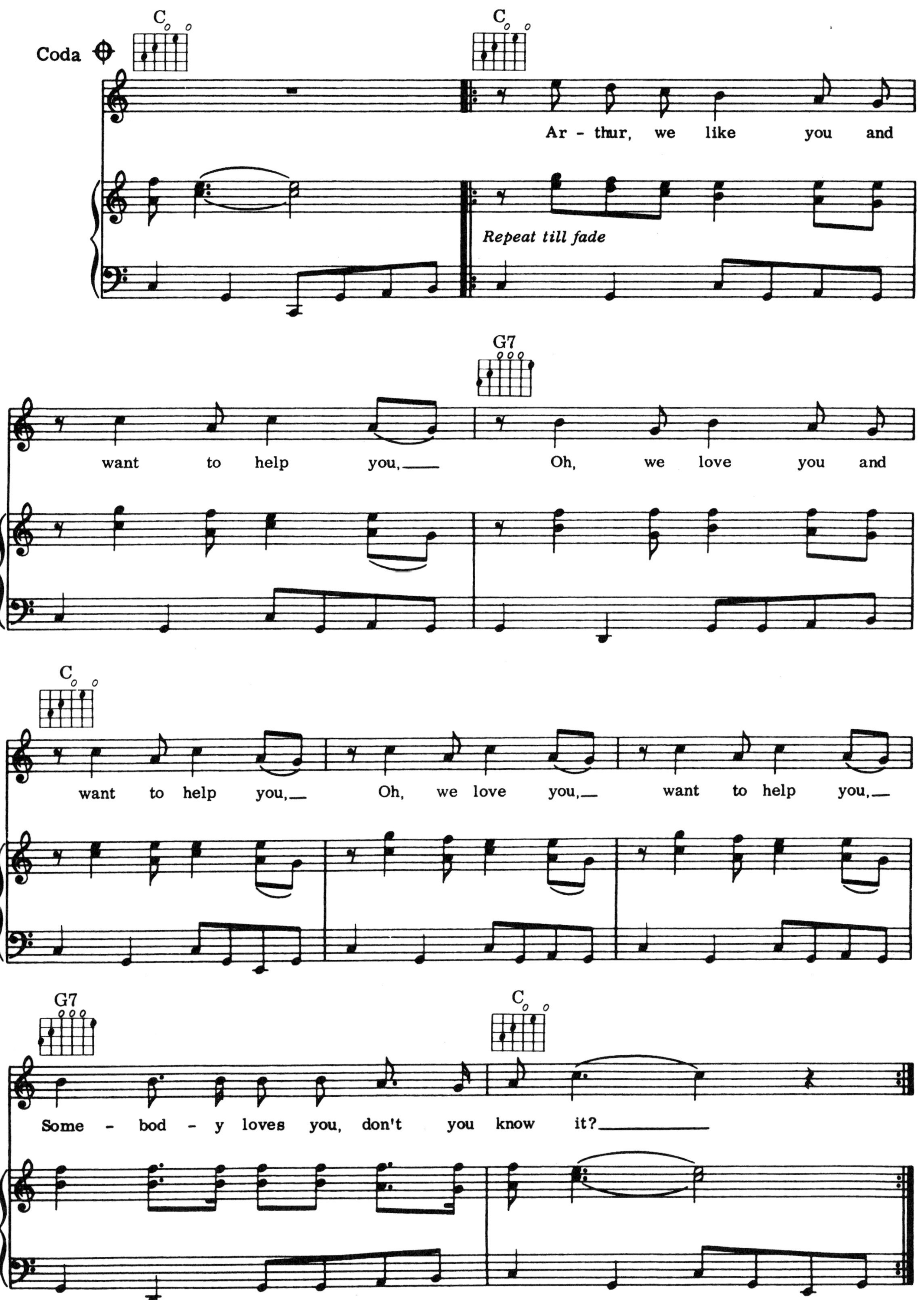

Coda
C
C
Repeat till fade
Ar - thur, we like you and
G7
want to help you,____ Oh, we love you and
C
want to help you,__ Oh, we love you,__ want to help you,__
G7
C
Some - bod - y loves you, don't you know it?__________

Autumn Almanac

Words & Music by Ray Davies

Moderato

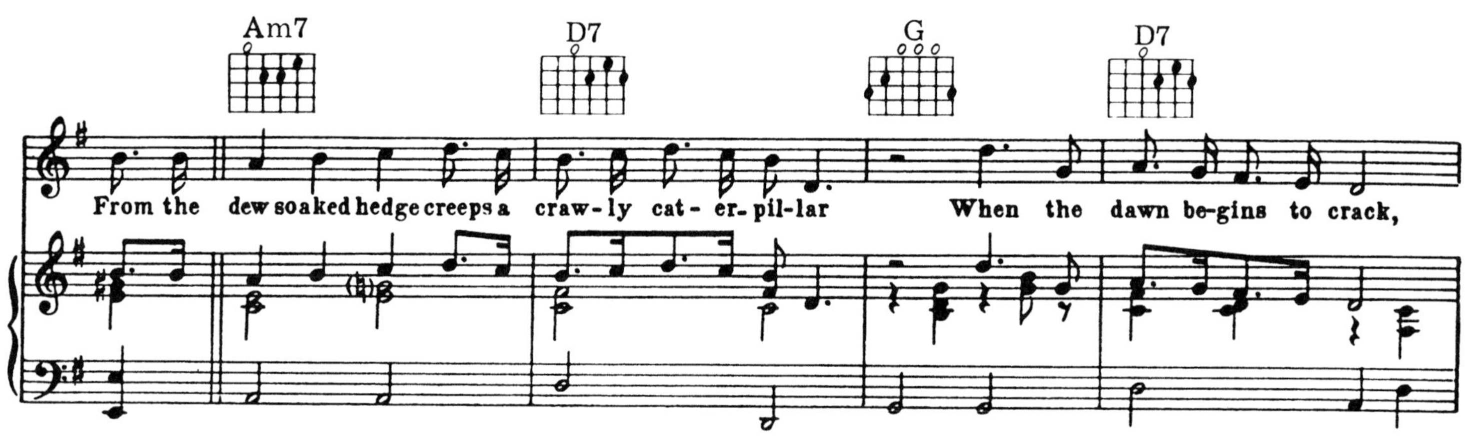

G   D7   C   D   G   D7   Em
So I sweep them in my sack, Yes, yes, yes, it's my Aut-umn Al-man-ac Fri-day ev'ning
E   A9   B7   E   A9   B7   E
peo - - ple get to - geth-er, Hid - ing from the wea-ther.
C#m   G#7   E   F#7
Tea and toast-ed, but-tered cur-rant buns,_ Will com-pen-sate for lack of sun_
Amaj7   Ab7   Am7   D7
_ Be-cause the sum-mer's all gone. La la la la la la la la la la la la la

G   D7   C   D   1 G   D7   2 G   D7
Oh! my poor rheumat-ic back! Yes, yes, yes, it's my Aut-umn Al-man-ac. Aut-umn Al-man-ac.
my Aut-umn Al-man-ac

G   D   C   G   D
I like my foot-ball   on a Sat-ur-day, Roast beef on Sun-day's

C   G   D   C   G   D   C   G
al-right. I go to Black-pool for my hol-i-days, Sit in the op-en sun-light.

Gm   Bb   Eb   F   F7   Bb
This is my street   and I'm nev-er gon-na leave it,   And I'm al-ways gon-na stay

Dm   Fm   G7   C   Cm
If I live to be nine - ty nine_ 'Cos all the peo-ple I meet_   Seem to come from the
G   E7   A7   B7   Em
street   And I can't get a - way   Be-cause it's call-ing me; Come on
B7   Em7   A7   Am7   D7
home,   come on home.   La la la la la la la la la la la la la
G   D7   C   D   G   D7
Repeat and fade
Oh! my Aut-umn Al - man-ac   Yes, yes, yes, it's my Aut-umn Al - man-ac.

Days

Words & Music by Ray Davies

I bless the light that lights on you be-lieve me And though you're
gone, you're with me ev-'ry sing le day, be-lieve me.
To Coda
Days I'll re-mem-ber all my life, Days when you can't see wrong from
right You took my life but then I knew that ve-ry soon you'd leave me
But it's al-right, now I'm not fright-ened of this world, be-lieve me.

F
A7
Dm
I wish to-day would be to-mor row, The night is dark
A7
Dm
C
Bb
it just brings sor-row let it wait.
A7
Thank you for the days.
D.S. al Coda
D
Ebmaj7
E7
F6
Days
CODA
F#7+
G
Ab
A
D

Dead End Street

Words & Music by Ray Davies

Am
G
F
living for
living for
Two roomed a - part - ment on the
Two roomed a - part - ment on the
E7
E7+
Am
G
sec - ond floor,
sec - ond floor,
No mon - ey com - in' in
No chance to em - i - grate
F
E7
E7+
A
The rent col - lec - tor's knock - ing trying to get in
I'm deep in debt - Now it's much too late
We are strict - ly
Peop - le want to
Dm
E7
sec - ond class and don't
work so hard we can't
un - der - stand.
get a chance.

Am
(Dead end) Why we should be on dead end street —— (Dead end) peop-le are liv-ing on
(Dead end) —— peop-le live in dead end street —— (Dead end) peop-le are dy- ing on
dead end street —— (Dead end) Have to live on dead end street, ——
dead end street —— (Dead end) I'm gon - na die on dead end street, ——
C   F
dead end street, —— (Yeah)
dead end street, —— (Yeah)
C   F
1
dead end street. —— (Yeah)
dead end street. —— (Yeah)
C   F   C   F   C   F
2
Dead end street, — (No)   Dead end street, — (Yeah)   That's my street, — (No)
(Repeat and fade.)

Dedicated Follower Of Fashion

Words & Music by Ray Davies

© Copyright 1966 Davray Music Limited.
Carlin Music Corporation, Iron Bridge House, 3 Bridge Approach, London NW1.
All Rights Reserved. International Copyright Secured.

C
F
It will make or break him so he's
C/G
E7/G#
A7
Dm
got to buy the best coz he's a de - di - ca - ted
G
C
1.
2, 3.
fol - low - er of fash - ion.
2. And when he does oh yes he is.
G7
C
(Oh yes he is.) Oh yes he is. (Oh yes he is.) He thinks

F   C
he is a flow-er to be looked at.   And

F   C/G   E7/G#   A7
when he pulls his frill-y ny-lon pant-ies right up tight he feels a

Dm   G   C
de-di-ca-ted fol-low-er of fash-ion.   Oh yes he is.

G7   C
(Oh yes he is.) Oh yes he is. (Oh yes he is.)   There's

one thing that he loves___ and that___ is flat-ter - y.
One week he's in pol - ka - dots,___ the next___ week he's in stripes coz he's___ a
de - di - ca - ted fol - low - er___ of fash - ion. 3. They seek him here,___
- ion. He's a de - di - ca - ted
To Coda
D.%. al Coda
Coda

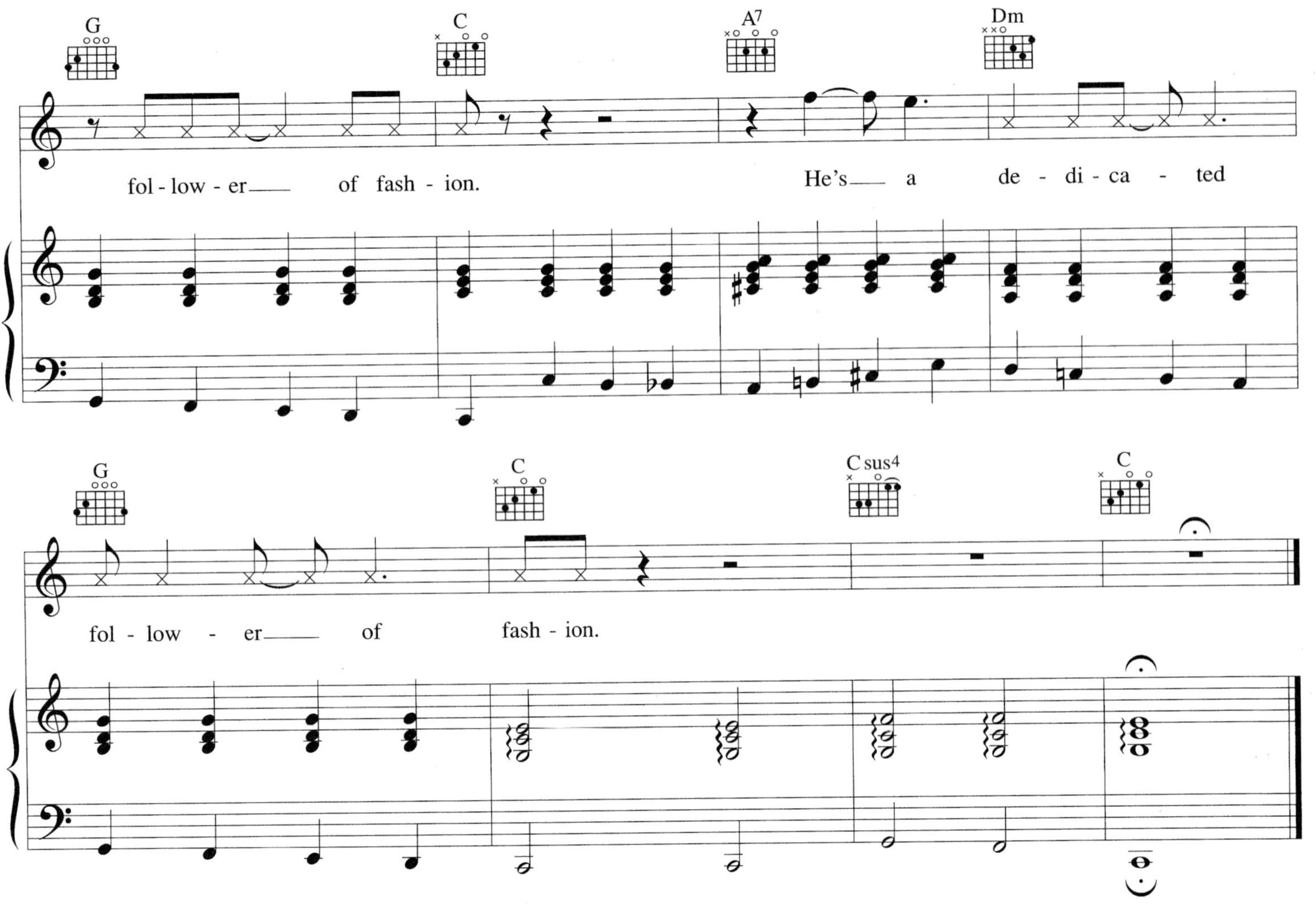

Verse 2:
And when he does
His little rounds
'Round the boutiques
Of London Town
Eagerly pursuing all the latest fads and trends
Coz he's a dedicated follower of fashion.

Oh yes he is *etc.*

Verse 3:
They seek him here
They seek him there
In Regent Street
And Leicester Square
Everywhere the Carnabitian Army marches on
Each one a dedicated follower of fashion.

Oh yes he is (oh yes he is)
Oh yes he is (oh yes he is)
His world is built 'round discoteques and parties
This pleasure seeking, individual always looks his best
Coz he's a dedicated follower of fashion
Oh yes he is (oh yes he is)
Oh yes he is (oh yes he is)
He flits from shop to shop just like a butterfly
In matters of the cloth he is as fickle as can be
Coz he's a dedicated follower of fashion.

Lola

Words & Music by Ray Davies

© Copyright 1970 Davray Music Limited.
Carlin Music Corporation, Iron Bridge House, 3 Bridge Approach, London NW1.
All Rights Reserved. International Copyright Secured.

E
walked up to me, and she asked me to dance____ I
I'm not dumb, but I can't un-der-stand____why she
A   D
asked her her name and in a dark brown voice____she said
walked like a wo-man and talked like a man oh my
E   A   D
Lo - la   El-oh-el - aye Lo - la   la la__ la la
Lo - la   la la__ la la Lo - la   la la__ la la
C   D   E
Lo - la.
Lo - la.

1
E
Well,

2
E
Well, we

B7
drank cham-pagne and danced all night___ Un - der e - lec-tric can - dle light,___ She

F#7

A
picked me up___ and sat me on her knee___ and said"Dear boy, won't you come home with me?"Well,

E
I'm not the world's most pas-sion-ate guy___ but when I

A   D
looked   in her eyes,   well, I   al - most   fell _____ for   my
E   A   D
Lo - la   la la ___ la la Lo - la   la la ___ la la
C   D   E
Lo - la.   Lo - la   la la ___ la la
A   D   C   D
Lo - la   la la ___ la la Lo - la.

E
A E B
A E B
A E B
E G#7 C#m
B B13 E
pushed her a-way, I walked to the door, I
fell to the floor, I got down on my knees then
I looked at her, and she at me. Well, that's the way that I want it to stay, and I
I

A
D
E
al-ways want it to be that way — for my Lo - la la la — la la
A
E
Lo - la. Girls will be boys, and boys — will be girls, it's a
A
D
E
mixed up, mud-dled up, shook up world — ex-cept for Lo - la la la — la la
A
B7
Lo - la. Well, I left home just a week be-fore — and

F#7
A
I'd ne-ver ev-er kissed a wo-man be-fore,___ But Lo - la smiled _ and took me by the hand ___ and
E
said "Dear boy, I'm gon-na make you a man.___ Well I'm not the world's most mas-cu-line man, But I
A
D
E
know what I am, and I'm glad I'm a man __ and so is Lo - la la la _ la la
Repeat and fade ad lib.
Lo - la la la _ la la Lo - la.

See My Friends

Words & Music by Ray Davies

See my friends, see my friends
E♭sus4
E♭
To Coda
play - ing a - cross the riv - er. She is gone,
Fm
she is gone and now there's no - one left, 'cept my
B♭
E♭sus4
E♭
friends play - ing a - cross the riv - er.

B♭m
E♭
fr3
A♭
fr4
Fm
B♭m
E♭
fr3
Fm/C
B♭
E♭sus4
E♭
fr3
D.%. al Coda
She is gone and now there's no - one else to
take her place. She is gone and now there's
no - one else to love, 'cept my friends
play - ing a - cross the riv - er.

Verse 2:
She just went
She just went
Went across the river
Now she's gone
Now she's gone
Wish that I'd gone with her
She is gone
She is gone
Is gone and now there's no-one left
'Cept my friends playing across the river.

Verse 3:
See my friends
See my friends playing across the river
She my friends
See my friends playing across the river.

Sunny Afternoon

Words & Music by Ray Davies

Dm
D7
SUN-NY AFT - ER - NOON.__
SUN-NY AFT - ER - NOON.__
Save me, save me,
Help me, help me,
G7
C7
save me from this squeeze,_______
help me sail a - way,_______
I've got a big fat mom-ma
You give me two good rea-sons
F
A7
Dm
tryin' to break __ me.
why I ought to stay.
And I love to live so
'Cause
G9
Dm
G7
C7
F
pleas-ant - ly,__
Live this life of lux - u - ry,_____
Laz - ing on a

SUN-NY AFT-ER-NOON,
In sum-mer-time,
In sum-mer-time,
In sum-mer-time,
to Coda
2. My
Ah
D.S. al Coda
CODA
In sum-mer-time,
In sum-mer-time,
(Tacet)
Repeat and fade

Till The End Of The Day

Words & Music by Ray Davies

C Dm F C Dm C
N.C.
Till the end of the day.___ Yeah!
N.C.
Dm C F C Dm C
2. You and me___ we live this life___
(Verse 3 see block lyric)
F C Dm C
from when we get up till we go sleep at night.
F A Dm
You and me, we're free.___

C   Dm   C   B♭
We do as we please, yes, from
F   G   B♭   A   1. C Dm F C Dm
morn - ing   till the end of the day.
(morn - ing   ooh.   )
C Dm F C Dm   C
N.C.
Till the end of the day.   Yeah!
2, 3.
Dm   C   Dm
To Coda
Till the end of the day.

C
Dm
Till the end of the day.
C
Dm
C
F
C
Till the end of the day.
Guitar solo
Dm
C
F
C
Dm
3
C
F
A
D.%. al Coda

Verse 3:
I get up and I see the sun up
I feel good yeah coz my life has begun.

You and me we're free *etc.*

Tired Of Waiting For You

Words & Music by Ray Davies

G6   F6/9   G6   F6/9   G6   F6/9
tired   of wait - ing— for— you.
F   C   F   C   F   C
I was a lone - ly soul,— I had no - bo - dy till— I met you.—
F   Gb   G   D7   G   D7
— But   you   keep - a me wait - ing   all of the time,
G   D7   G   D7   G
— what can I do?—   It's your life—

Bm
F
D7
and you can do what you want.
G
Bm
F
Do what you like but please don't keep-a me wait-
D
F
D7
-ing, please don't keep-a me wait - ing coz I'm
G
F
G
F
G
F
so tired, tired of wait-ing, tired of wait-ing for

G   F   G   F   G   F
you. So tired,—
G   F   G   F   G   F
tired of wait - ing, tired of wait - ing— for— you.—
G   F   G   F   G   F
For you.— For
G   F   G   F   G
you.—

You Really Got Me

Words & Music by Ray Davies

© Copyright 1964 Edward Kassner Music Company Limited, Exmouth House, 11 Pine Street, London EC1.
All Rights Reserved. International Copyright Secured.

58

G5 F5 G5 F5 G5 F5 G5 A5 G5 A5 G5
so I can't sleep at night.— Yeah, you real - ly
(8vb)
A5 G5 A5 G5 A5 G5 A5 G5
got me now, you got me so I don't know what I'm do - ing——
A5 G5 A5 C D C D C D C D C
—— now. Oh yeah, you real - ly got me now, you got me
D C D C D C D C D C
so I can't sleep at night. You real - ly got me,— you real - ly got me,— you

To Coda
1.
D
C
D
C
real - ly got me.
2.
G5
F5
G5
F5
G5
F5
G5
F5
G5
F5
G5
F5
G5
F5
G5
F5
G5
F5
G5
F5

Verses 2 & 3 (%):
See, don't ever set me free
I always want to be by your side.
Girl, you really got me now,
You got me so I can't sleep at night.
Yeah, you really got me now,
You got me so I don't know what I'm doing now.
Oh yeah, you really got me now,
You got me so I can't sleep at night.
You really got me.

Waterloo Sunset

Words & Music by Ray Davies

© Copyright 1967 Davray Music Limited.
Carlin Music Corporation, Iron Bridge House, 3 Bridge Approach, London NW1.
All Rights Reserved. International Copyright Secured.

Fm
C
Fm7
need no   friends
feel a - fraid
need no   friends
Bb
Eb
To Coda
Bb
as long as I gaze   on Wat-er-loo sun - set I am in par-
as long as I gaze   on Wat-er-loo sun - set I am in par-
as long as they gaze   on Wat-er-loo sun - set they are in par-
Ab
C7
F
- a - dise
- a - dise
- a - dise
Ev'-ry day I
Bb
C7
F
look at the world from my   win - dow

F
Bb7
The chil-ly, chil-li-est eve ___ ning time ___ Wat-er-loo sun - set's fine ___
(Wat-er-loo sun - set's fine) ___
Ter-ry meets Ju-
Mil-lions of peo- D.%. al Coda
CODA
Bb
Ab
Bb
___ -set I am in par - a - dise
Bb7
Ebmaj7
Wat-er-loo sun - set's fine ___ (Wat-er-loo sun - sets fine.) ___